A
Christmas
Sampler
of Feasts

CHRISTMAS
is a season of feasts shared
joyously with family
and friends. From cookbooks
by many Doubleday authors
we have assembled a
sampler of menus
with recipes that should recall
glorious past celebrations
and provide new,
equally delectable culinary
adventures.

A
Christmas
Sampler
of Feasts

MENUS AND RECIPES
FOR THE
TWELVE DAYS OF
CHRISTMAS.

Compilation and Art Direction
by Diana Klemin.
Drawings by Mona Mark

DOUBLEDAY & COMPANY, INC.
Garden City, New York, 1982

WE GRATEFULLY ACKNOWLEDGE
the following for permission to reprint their copyrighted material:

"Baked Apples," "Brioche (Easy Method)," "Roast Leg of Lamb Stuffed with Rice, Piñon Nuts, and Currants," "Quiche Lorraine," "Poached Salmon," "Sauce Verte," "Homemade Mayonnaise," and "Rice Pilaf" are all from THE DOUBLEDAY COOKBOOK by Jean Anderson and Elaine Hanna. Copyright © 1975 by Doubleday & Company, Inc.

"Scrambled Eggs," "Roast Turkey with Prune and Pork Sausage Stuffing," "Braised Chestnuts," "Heart of Lettuce and Heart of Romaine Salad," "French Dressing with Mustard," "Chicken in Tarragon Aspic," "Chicken Bouillon," "Chicken Consommé," "Clarifying Consommé," and "Lettuce Salad with Orange" are all from FRENCH CUISINE FOR ALL by Louisette Bertholle, translated by Mary Manheim. English Translation copyright © 1980 by Doubleday & Company, Inc.

"Cranberry Conserve" is from THE GOOD FOOD COMPENDIUM by Jo Giese Brown. Copyright © 1981 by Jo Giese Brown.

"Orkney Islands Plum Pudding," "Drambuie or Brandy Sauce," "Claret Consommé," and "Very Rich Chocolate Cake" are from FOOD IN VOGUE by Maxime de La Falaise. Copyright © 1942, 1946, 1948, 1950, 1955, 1958, 1960, 1963, 1968, 1969, 1970, 1971, 1972, 1973, 1974, 1975, 1976 and 1981 by The Condé Nast Publications Inc.

"Roast Goose with Potato and Bread Stuffing," "Tomato and Eggplant Casserole," "Gingerbread with Lemon-Rum Sauce," "Chocolate Soufflé," "Meringue-Nut Kisses," "Hot Mince Pie," "Sour Cream and Potato Soup," "Baked Home-Cured Ham with Wine-Raisin Sauce," "Superb Sweet Potatoes," "Turnips, Rutabaga, and Kohlrabi," "Waldorf Salad," and "Funny Pie" are all from BETTY GROFF'S COUNTRY GOODNESS COOKBOOK. Copyright © 1981 by Betty Groff.

"Pilaf with Artichokes" and "Chestnut Cake with Whipped Cream" are from REGIONAL CUISINES OF GREECE by The Recipe Club of St. Paul's Greek Orthodox Church. Copyright © 1981 by The Recipe Club of St. Paul's Greek Orthodox Church of Hempstead, New York.

LIBRARY OF CONGRESS CATALOGING IN PUBLICATION DATA
MAIN ENTRY UNDER TITLE:
A Christmas sampler of feasts.
Includes index.
1. Christmas cookery. I. Klemin, Diana.
TX39.C487 1982   641.5'68   AACR2
Library of Congress Catalog Card Number: 82-45447

CONTENTS

SHRIMP COCKTAIL WITH HOT SAUCE

CHEESE BISCUITS

ROAST GOOSE WITH POTATO AND
BREAD STUFFING*

MASHED POTATOES

TOMATO AND EGGPLANT
CASSEROLE*

BROCCOLI WITH CHEESE SAUCE

GREENS WITH CREAMY
SWEET-SOUR DRESSING

GINGERBREAD* WITH
LEMON-RUM SAUCE*

CHOCOLATE SOUFFLÉ*

MERINGUE-NUT KISSES*

*Starred recipes appear in the text—see Index

Christmas Eve Dinner

OUR CHRISTMAS EVE DINNER is always very traditional. I like to cook it myself as long as I have the strength. I hope I can continue to have Christmas dinner with my family on Christmas Eve. To me, the perfect way to spend Christmas Eve is with my family—all the children and grandchildren. At that time, we talk over the blessings of the past year and exchange our gifts. Then on Christmas morning we discuss the Christmas story one more time and we are grateful for another good season.

My family tells me what each would like to have for Christmas Eve dinner. As a result, the dinner does not necessarily turn out to be one where everything blends together, or one where everything is cooked on the top of the stove, or is all done in the oven. But it is a dinner that just seems right for the occasion. Our family loves roast goose with a special stuffing and other dishes I am featuring in this menu.

Gingerbread with Lemon-Rum Sauce is an excellent dessert, and it gives that special holiday spirit, much like plum pudding.

Just a hint for the Chocolate Soufflé. It adds a special touch. Be assured that Chocolate Soufflé is not too difficult to make. As a matter of fact, one Christmas Eve I dropped it on the floor. Luckily, it did not turn over, so I picked it up and put it back in the oven. It baked perfectly and we were able to serve it with no problems. So forget that myth about having to breathe quietly around a Chocolate Soufflé.

from BETTY GROFF'S COUNTRY GOODNESS COOKBOOK

ROAST GOOSE WITH POTATO AND BREAD STUFFING

SERVES 6
1 (8-pound) fresh dressed goose
Salt
Pepper
1 recipe Potato and Bread Stuffing (given below)
2 cups water

GRAVY

2 cups water
2 tablespoons cornstarch
¼ cup cold water

Wash the goose and sprinkle salt and pepper inside the bird. Fill with potato and bread stuffing. Liberally salt and pepper the outside. After securing the stuffed cavity with skewers, place the bird, breast side down, on a wire rack in a roasting pan. Add the water and cover, or tent with foil. Roast in a preheated 350° F. oven for 5 hours. Remove the cover and turn breast side up, for browning, for the last 30 minutes.

Bake the extra stuffing in a buttered dish for the last 30 minutes of the baking time for the goose.

Make gravy by removing fat, adding 2 cups water to brownings, and thickening with 2 tablespoons cornstarch dissolved in ¼ cup water. Stir over low heat until all the brownings have dissolved and the mixture has thickened.

POTATO AND BREAD STUFFING

½ cup water
½ cup chopped celery with leaves
¼ cup chopped onion
1 teaspoon salt
¼ teaspoon ground pepper
1 tablespoon chopped parsley
Pinch saffron
2 cups mashed potatoes
3 eggs, lightly beaten
2 cups fresh bread cubes
1 cup milk

Put the water in a 1-quart saucepan and bring to a boil. Add the celery, onion, salt, pepper, parsley, and saffron. Boil approximately 7 minutes until the celery is clear. Lightly mix the celery mixture with the potatoes, beaten eggs, bread cubes, and milk in a large bowl. If used as a side dish, bake in a buttered dish in a preheated 350° F. oven for 30 minutes.

TOMATO AND EGGPLANT CASSEROLE

SERVES 6

One winter, Abe and I took a Caribbean vacation at the Golden Lemon on St. Kitts, owned by our good friend Arthur Leaman. We spent our time eating and relaxing—wonderful, when someone else is cooking. Arthur's cook put freshly grated nutmeg on top of this casserole, giving it another flavor entirely. Tomato and eggplant make a delicate and delicious combination. I have made this recipe without tomatoes and used it as eggplant stuffing for a turkey. Turkey tends to be dry, but the eggplant adds a lovely moistness. There are many ways to use a good recipe!

1 medium eggplant
1 tablespoon finely chopped onion
1½ teaspoons salt
2 tablespoons butter
2 eggs, beaten
¼ teaspoon freshly ground black pepper
½ teaspoon oregano
½ cup dry bread crumbs
1 large tomato, cored and cut into 6 medium-thick slices
½ cup grated Cheddar cheese

Peel the eggplant and slice ¼" thick. Put in a saucepan with the onion, salt, and ½" boiling water. Cover and simmer about 10 minutes until tender. Drain well and mash. Blend in the butter, eggs, pepper, oregano, and bread crumbs. Turn into a buttered 1½-quart casserole. Cover with the tomato slices. Sprinkle with the cheese and salt and pepper. Bake in a preheated 375° F. oven for 25 minutes until lightly browned.

11

GINGERBREAD

SERVES 12

⅜ cup butter

⅜ cup vegetable shortening

2 cups light brown sugar

3 eggs

*1 cup thick milk or buttermilk (add 1 tablespoon lemon juice
    to the milk to make it thick and let stand 5 minutes)*

1 teaspoon salt

1 teaspoon baking soda

1 teaspoon ground cinnamon

1 teaspoon ground ginger

1 teaspoon ground nutmeg

3¾ cups flour

¾ cup molasses

Lemon-Rum Sauce (given below) or whipped cream

In a large mixing bowl, cream the butter, shortening, and brown sugar. Gradually add the eggs and thick milk. In a smaller bowl, combine the salt, soda, cinnamon, ginger, nutmeg, and flour. Gradually add the flour mixture and the molasses, alternately, to the egg mixture. Blend well. Pour this batter into a greased and floured 9"×13" baking pan. Bake in a preheated 350° F. oven for 1 hour. Serve with lemon-rum sauce or whipped cream.

LEMON-RUM SAUCE

SERVES 12

1 cup sugar
¼ teaspoon salt
1 tablespoon flour
2½ tablespoons cornstarch
2 cups water
Grated rind 1 lemon
2 tablespoons butter
4 tablespoons lemon juice
1 cup rum

In a heavy 2-quart saucepan, mix the sugar, salt, flour, and cornstarch. Slowly add the water, mixing until smooth. Place over medium heat and bring to a boil, stirring constantly. Add the grated lemon rind. Reduce heat to low and simmer for 7 minutes. Add butter, lemon juice, and rum, and stir once more. Serve hot.

CHOCOLATE SOUFFLÉ

SERVES 4−6

3 tablespoons butter
2½ tablespoons flour
1¼ cups milk
½ cup granulated sugar
½ teaspoon salt
3 tablespoons cocoa
5 egg yolks
1 teaspoon vanilla extract
5 egg whites, stiffly beaten
Butter
Granulated sugar for sprinkling

In a 1-quart saucepan, melt the butter over medium heat. Add the flour and stir until smooth. Slowly add the milk, continuing to stir. Gradually add the sugar, salt, and cocoa. Cook until the sauce is smooth and thick, stirring constantly. Remove from heat and cool slightly. Beat the egg yolks. Add yolks and the vanilla to the sauce, stirring until well blended. Fold the stiffly beaten egg whites into the sauce. Pour the mixture into a 1½-quart straight-sided soufflé dish which has been generously buttered and sprinkled with sugar. Set the dish in a pan of hot water and bake in a preheated 450° F. oven, on the low rack, for 15 minutes. Reduce the heat to 375° F. and bake 25 minutes more. Serve immediately.

MERINGUE-NUT KISSES

MAKES 3 DOZEN

⅛ cup egg whites
¼ teaspoon cream of tartar
2 cups sifted confectioners' sugar
¼ teaspoon salt
1 cup coarsely broken unsalted nutmeats (pecans, shellbarks, or walnuts)
½ teaspoon vanilla extract

Beat the egg whites and cream of tartar in a large mixing bowl until they form soft peaks. Sift together the sugar and salt and gradually beat into the egg whites. Beat until they hold stiff peaks. Fold in the nutmeats and vanilla. Drop mixture by teaspoonfuls onto greased cookie sheets and bake 1 sheet at a time. Preheat the oven to 375° F. When ready to bake kisses, reduce the heat to 350° F. and bake 7–8 minutes. The peaks should be a pale golden. Do not overbake. The kisses should be dry on the outside, moist on the inside. Cool thoroughly before packing in airtight containers. These freeze well.

BAKED APPLES★

SCRAMBLED EGGS★

PAN-FRIED CANADIAN BACON

CROISSANTS

BRIOCHE★

MARMALADE

SWEET BUTTER

COFFEE

Christmas Morn

CHRISTMAS BREAKFAST should not be overlooked. Simple and festive, it is balm to the soul after the last present has been opened. These spiced apples from *The Doubleday Cookbook* have a special Christmas look.

BAKED APPLES

SERVES 4

4 large baking apples
⅔ cup sugar
⅔ cup water
1 tablespoon butter or margarine
Pinch cinnamon and/or nutmeg
2 – 3 drops red food coloring

Preheat oven to 350° F. Core apples, then peel about ⅓ of the way down from the stem end, or, if you prefer, peel entirely. Arrange in an ungreased shallow baking pan. Boil remaining ingredients about 5 minutes to form a clear syrup, pour over apples, and bake uncovered ¾ – 1 hour, basting often with syrup, until crisp-tender. Serve hot or cold, topped if you like with custard sauce or whipped cream.

SCRAMBLED EGGS

SERVES 3
3 tablespoons butter plus 2 – 3 pats of cold butter
10 very fresh eggs
A few drops of water (no more than a teaspoon)
Salt
Freshly ground white pepper

Melt the butter in the saucepan or in the top of a double boiler. Crack the eggs into a large bowl, add the water, salt, and pepper. Beat the eggs rapidly with a fork until the yolks and whites are just blended. Pour the eggs into the saucepan, place on top of the simmering water over moderate heat. With a wooden spatula stir the eggs with a smooth, wide, regular, circular motion, the spatula touching the bottom of the pan. For 1 or 2 minutes nothing will seem to happen, the mixture will not seem to be thickening. With patience, continue to work with the spatula without increasing speed, and suddenly the eggs will start to thicken and a few lumps will appear. Stir a little faster, scraping down the bits of egg on the sides of the pan. Remove it from the heat, and with a whisk beat in the pats of cold butter one after the other. This will stop the cooking and make the eggs shine. Place the eggs immediately onto a warmed metal dish, then serve on warmed plates.

BRIOCHE
(EASY METHOD)

MAKES 2 DOZEN

1 package active dry yeast

¼ cup warm water (105 –15° F.)

4 cups sifted flour

3 tablespoons sugar

1 teaspoon salt

1½ cups butter or margarine, softened to room temperature

6 eggs, lightly beaten

1 egg yolk, lightly beaten with 1 tablespoon cold water (glaze)

Mix yeast, warm water, and ¼ cup flour until smooth in a small bowl; set in a pan of lukewarm water (water should come ⅓ of way up bowl) and let stand in a warm spot until bubbles form on yeast mixture, 5–10 minutes. Meanwhile, sift 3 cups flour with the sugar and salt and set aside. Cream butter in a large bowl with an electric mixer until fluffy. Add flour mixture, a little at a time, alternately with eggs. Beat 2 minutes at medium speed. Add yeast mixture, beat ½ minute at low speed, then 2 minutes at medium speed. Add remaining ¾ cup flour by hand, a little at a time, beating with a wooden spoon after each addition. Cover dough with cloth, set in a warm, draft-free spot, and let rise until doubled in bulk, 2½–3 hours. Stir dough down, cover with foil, and refrigerate 6–8 hours or overnight. Dough will rise slightly and become quite firm. Scrape dough onto a lightly floured board, knead lightly with floured hands, and shape quickly into a ball. Cut ball in 4 equal pieces with a floured knife and cut 3 of the quarters into 8 pieces, totaling 24. Roll into smooth balls and place in greased brioche or muffin pans, 1 ball per cup. With dampened index finger, make a deep depression in center of each ball. Roll remaining dough into 24 small balls and place 1 in each depression to form the "topknot." Cover brioches, set in a warm spot, and let rise until doubled in bulk, about 1 hour. About 15 minutes before you're ready to bake, preheat oven to 425° F., set rack in lower ⅓ of oven. Gently brush brioches with glaze, taking care not to let it run into cracks around top-knots (an artist's brush is best). Set pans on baking sheets and bake 12−15 minutes until well browned. Remove from pans at once after baking and serve hot or, if you prefer, cool on wire racks to room temperature.

HEARTS OF PALM

ROAST TURKEY

WITH PRUNE AND PORK

SAUSAGE STUFFING*

BOILED ONIONS

BRAISED CHESTNUTS*

STRING BEANS

MASHED POTATOES

CRANBERRY CONSERVE*

ORKNEY ISLANDS

PLUM PUDDING*

WITH DRAMBUIE OR BRANDY SAUCE*

HOT MINCE PIE*

Christmas Dinner

TRADITIONAL ROAST TURKEY with a French accent adds flair to the best dinner of the year.

TURKEY
DINDE

TRANSLATOR'S NOTE: In France turkeys are much smaller than in the United States. Big turkeys are almost nonexistent. According to Mme. Bertholle, the traditional turkey stuffing contains truffles, but she is of the opinion that the fine savor of turkey tends to be lost when it is mingled with the wonderful but overpowering taste and aroma of truffles. She also admits that truffles in the stuffing these days are a wild extravagance, and one we can easily live without. She very kindly supplies us with a recipe *sans truffes* that is as delicious and original as it is thrifty.

ROAST TURKEY WITH PRUNE AND PORK SAUSAGE STUFFING
DINDE RÔTIE AUX PRUNEAUX ET AUX CHIPOLATAS

SERVES 4–6

A wonderfully savory dish to set before your guests on Christmas Day! If it comes as a disappointment that the truffle-colored prunes are not really truffles, just taste—you will find they are a delicious disappointment.

Remember that turkeys must be basted frequently, not with the pan juices, but with melted butter kept warm in a small saucepan.

For cooking the turkey, you will need a large roasting pan equipped with a rack and a large oval heavy-bottomed enameled casserole with a cover.

1 pound "tenderized" prunes
1½ cups hot tea
1½ tablespoons cognac
Butter for the skillet
1 pound small link pork sausages plus a little more butter
    for browning them
1 turkey liver
Salt
Freshly ground pepper
1 ready-to-cook, young, 7−9-pound turkey, neck cut off and
    set aside with giblets
3 strips barding fat, each 3 fingers wide, for tying on drum-
    sticks and breast
Oil for the roasting pan
3−4 tablespoons margarine, cut in small pieces
4 tablespoons hot water placed in with turkey (optional)
5−8 tablespoons butter, kept warm in a small pan
½ cup hot water for deglazing the roasting pan

Preheat oven to 350° F. Macerate the prunes in the hot tea flavored with ½ tablespoon of the cognac until they are plump and soft. Drain, pit, and pat dry.

Butter a skillet and lightly brown the sausages. They should not be completely cooked, just relieved of some of their fat. Drain on paper towels and allow to cool completely.

Cut the turkey liver into 4−6 pieces and marinate for a few minutes in the 1 tablespoon of cognac, remove, and pat dry. Reserve the cognac.

Salt and pepper the inside of the turkey and stuff it with the prunes, sausages, and liver. Sew up or skewer the opening. Tie the barding fat around the drumsticks and breast. Truss the turkey.

Grease the roasting pan with oil and distribute the pieces of margarine. Place the turkey, breast side up, on the rack. The hot water may be added at this time.

Melt the butter and keep it warm. Roast the turkey for 20 minutes, basting frequently with melted butter. Turn the turkey on its side, roast for another 20 minutes, continuing to baste. Repeat the process for the other side.

Transfer the turkey to the casserole. Remove the barding fat. Deglaze the cooking juices in the roasting pan with the ½ cup of hot water, strain into the casserole. Cover the turkey loosely with aluminum foil. Set the cover on slightly askew, cook the turkey either over moderate heat on top of the stove or in the oven turned down to 300° F. for at least 1 hour, or until the juices run a clear amber color when the fleshy part of the leg is pricked.

TURKEY STOCK SERVED AS A SAUCE
JUS DE DINDE

MAKES ABOUT 1½ – 2 CUPS

Make a stock, using about 3 cups of the turkey neck, cut in 3 pieces, and the giblets, which have been marinated in the remainder of the 1 tablespoon of cognac for 10 minutes. Strain the stock into a small saucepan and degrease. Taste and adjust seasoning.

SERVING THE TURKEY

Transfer the turkey to a board and let it rest for 10 minutes before carving it. Cut the breast meat into thin slices and arrange on a warmed large metal platter with the rest of the pieces. Garnish the platter with the prunes and sausages. Heat the sauce and pour it into a warmed sauce bowl.

CHESTNUTS
MARRONS

This delicious, mealy vegetable evokes Christmas goose or turkey for most of us. But chestnuts are also excellent, either braised or puréed, with all sorts of game. Many home cooks hesitate to make chestnuts because of the chore of peeling them. Here is a simple, quick way to perform this supposedly horrendous task.

Preheat oven to 400° F. Make 2 gashes on the flat side of each chestnut. Place chestnuts on a dripping pan and put in the oven for 4–5 minutes. (Note: If the chestnuts are freshly gathered, leave them in the oven for only 3 minutes.) Remove the chestnuts from the oven, shell, and peel.

BASIC METHOD FOR COOKING CHESTNUTS

Chestnuts tend to fall apart when cooked in water or milk. If you wish to make whole chestnuts, follow this method: Cook them in chicken or veal stock (to cover) that has been bound by a small amount of flour or arrowroot diluted in water. This keeps the chestnuts from disintegrating.

BRAISED CHESTNUTS
MARRONS BRAISÉS

SERVES 6
Butter for the oven dish
2¼ cups veal bouillon or chicken bouillon
2 teaspoons arrowroot or flour dissolved in a little
*   cold water*
30 large raw chestnuts, peeled
3 tablespoons butter, cut in small pieces
1 bouquet garni *with a piece of fennel and a*
*   small celery leaf*
Small amount salt
Freshly ground pepper

Preheat oven to 350° F. Butter a shallow oven dish large enough to hold all the chestnuts in one layer. Heat the bouillon in a separate pan and stir in the dissolved arrowroot or flour.

Arrange the chestnuts in the oven dish, pour in the bouillon so that the chestnuts are just barely covered. Sprinkle on the pieces of butter, add the *bouquet garni*, and season with a little salt and pepper. Cover the dish with a piece of aluminum foil, place in the oven for about 45 minutes, basting once or twice, and checking the level of the bouillon, adding a little more if necessary. At the end of cooking, the chestnuts should be whole and tender.

CRANBERRY CONSERVE

MAKES ABOUT 5 CUPS

Every year in the fall, as Thanksgiving approaches, I traditionally make cranberry conserve. I usually multiply the recipe many times to make enough to see me and my friends through the holidays and into spring. I put this into Mason jars, and keep them refrigerated. It goes wonderfully with turkey and poultry, but also try it with beef. If you compare cost, my cranberry conserve is probably double the cost of the canned variety, but you'd never bring a can of that to someone's house as a present and this makes a perfect gift.

1 pound fresh cranberries
1 cup water
½ cup sugar or ¼ cup honey
½ cup raisins
1 orange, cut into chunky pieces
½ cup sliced pineapple (optional)
½ cup chopped walnuts

Bring the berries to boil in the water and simmer till they pop open (about 3−5 minutes), but watch that they are still firm and not getting mushy.

Stir in sugar, raisins, orange pieces. Simmer for about 15 minutes. If you like your conserve extra sweet, you could add ½ cup pineapple slices, but I think the pineapple detracts from the special tart taste of the cranberry. If this is too tart for you, add more sweet oranges, or a dash more sugar, but be prepared for this to taste boldly of cranberries and not of cranberries in sugary syrup the way the canned product does.

At this stage, your house is filled with the most wonderful fragrance. It's probably worth it to make cranberry conserve just for the side benefit of the wonderful scents that waft through the rooms.

Stir in the walnuts. The ½ cup is enough, but I usually add extra for more crunch.

If you compare nutrition, we've made this recipe more flavorful and nutritious than its commercial counterpart by adding the raisins and nuts. The vitamin C that was in the raw berry was approximately 10 mg per cup; this has been cut to approximately 6 mg by the cooking process, but since cranberries are never eaten in their raw form, it doesn't serve much purpose to compare them to an unobtainable ideal.

Be prepared for this to grow on you as this mixture improves with age. With age might come mold, also, although the sugar content combined with the acid content usually will safeguard against the formation of mold. If you do notice some mold, it's not toxic; don't go overboard and feel you have to sacrifice the whole container of delicious cranberry conserve. With a clean instrument (a knife is easiest), scrape away the mold and be careful not to contaminate the other parts. (However, if you ever notice mold on breads, nuts, or cereals, that mold is toxic and the food should be thrown away immediately.)

ORKNEY ISLANDS PLUM PUDDING

SERVES 8–10
1 cup stone-ground whole-wheat flour
1 teaspoon baking soda
4 cups stale whole-wheat bread crumbs
8 ounces seedless raisins
8 ounces suet, finely chopped
1 cup raw sugar (found at health food stores)
Dark beer or ale
1 egg, beaten
All-purpose flour, as needed

Sift the whole-wheat flour with the soda; mix with the crumbs, raisins, suet, and sugar. Add enough beer to make a soft dough. Knead in the egg. Dip a dish towel into boiling water, wring it out, sprinkle with flour, and line a greased porcelain pudding bowl with it, floured side up. Turn the dough into the bowl, gather the towel and tie it with string, allowing room for expansion. Put the bowl on a rack in a large pot, fill pot with boiling water almost to the top of the bowl. Simmer gently, uncovered, 4 hours, adding more boiling water to maintain the original level. Unmold and serve hot with the following sauce, made with Drambuie or brandy.

DRAMBUIE OR BRANDY SAUCE

MAKES 3 CUPS, SERVES 8–10

1 tablespoon flour
6 tablespoons sweet (unsalted) butter
1 tablespoon sugar
1½ cups boiling water
½ cup Drambuie or brandy

Toast the flour in a small heavy saucepan, stirring over low heat, until light brown. Blend with the butter. Dissolve the sugar in the boiling water, stir slowly into the flour-butter mixture, simmer 10 minutes. Add the Drambuie or brandy and serve hot.

HOT MINCE PIE

Making a good mincemeat is so much work that it is a sensible idea to make enough at one time to last an entire season. It freezes or cans well, even in pie crust, but I prefer to make my pies fresh each time.

MINCEMEAT

MAKES ABOUT 8 QUARTS

5 pounds lean hamburger
2 quarts dried apples, soaked
5 pounds fresh apples, cored and peeled
4 lemons
1 pound raisins
1 pound currants, or raisins if currants are unavailable
1½ pounds light brown sugar
1 quart light table molasses
1 cup cider vinegar

3 cups strong-flavored wine
1 teaspoon ground cinnamon
1 teaspoon grated nutmeg
1 teaspoon ground cloves
½ teaspoon ground mace

Cook the hamburger in a heavy skillet over medium heat, breaking it up with a wooden spoon, until all traces of pink have disappeared. The meat should be cooked through but not browned.

Grind the soaked dried apples and fresh apples coarsely in a meat grinder or food processor. Grind the lemons, peel and all. This may be done in a blender.

Combine the hamburger, ground fruit, and remaining ingredients in a heavy pot. Bring to a boil. Reduce the heat and simmer for 30 minutes, stirring to combine well. Ladle into sterilized quart jars, cool, and seal. Or pack in plastic containers and freeze.

TO MAKE A MINCE PIE

SERVES 4–6 GENEROUSLY
Pastry for 2 (9") crusts
2½ cups mincemeat
½ cup wine or whiskey

Divide pastry dough in half. Roll out 1 crust. Place in a 9" piepan. Fill crust with mincemeat and wine. Roll out the remaining dough and slit it, making a design, to let the steam escape. Moisten the edges of the pastry, then top pie with slit crust. Crimp the edges to seal. Bake in a preheated 350° F. oven for approximately 45 minutes until juice bubbles out of pierced holes in top. Serve hot.

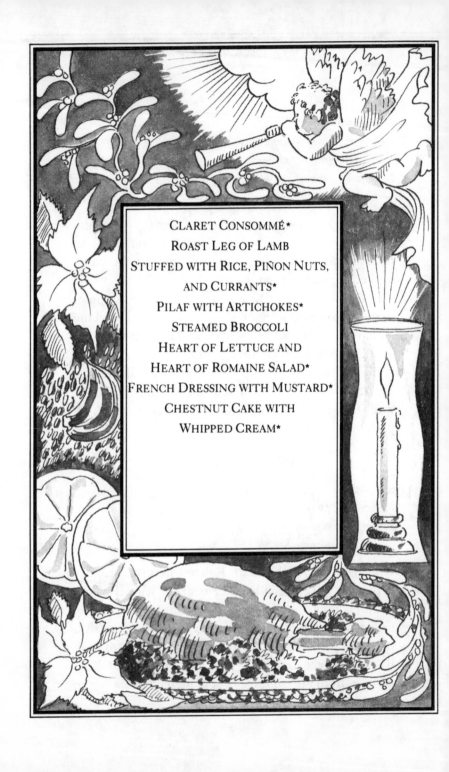

CLARET CONSOMMÉ*
ROAST LEG OF LAMB
STUFFED WITH RICE, PIÑON NUTS,
AND CURRANTS*
PILAF WITH ARTICHOKES*
STEAMED BROCCOLI
HEART OF LETTUCE AND
HEART OF ROMAINE SALAD*
FRENCH DRESSING WITH MUSTARD*
CHESTNUT CAKE WITH
WHIPPED CREAM*

New Year's Eve Dinner

I N AMERICA, NEW YEAR'S EVE is a continuation of the celebration of Christmas, a wonderful time to entertain friends or gather the family together.

CLARET CONSOMMÉ

SERVES 6
1½ cups claret wine
1 small cinnamon stick
1 tablespoon sugar
1 quart chicken or beef consommé
1 lemon, thinly sliced

Heat the claret with the cinnamon stick and sugar, simmer 10 minutes. Remove the cinnamon stick. Add the consommé, heat. Garnish each serving with a thin slice of lemon.

ROAST LEG OF LAMB STUFFED WITH RICE, PIÑON NUTS, AND CURRANTS

SERVES 6−8

1 (6-pound) leg of lamb

STUFFING

2 tablespoons olive oil
½ cup uncooked rice
1 medium-size yellow onion, peeled and minced
1 clove garlic, peeled and crushed
3 tablespoons minced fresh parsley
1 tablespoon minced fresh mint
¼ cup dried currants
½ cup piñon nuts
1 cup chicken broth
1 teaspoon salt
¼ teaspoon pepper

Ask butcher to bone leg of lamb, leaving about 2″ of leg bone in at the narrow end (this makes the leg handsomer and easier to stuff).

Preheat oven to 325° F. For stuffing, heat oil 1 minute in a saucepan over moderately high heat, add rice, onion, and garlic, and stir-fry 2−3 minutes until rice is golden. Mix in remaining ingredients, cover, and simmer 8−10 minutes until all moisture is absorbed. Cool slightly. Spoon stuffing into leg, then sew or skewer cavity shut. Place leg in a large shallow roasting pan and roast, uncovered, 3 hours. To carve, cut straight across in ½″ slices.

PILAF WITH ARTICHOKES
PILAFI ME ANGINARES

SERVES 10–12

4 tablespoons butter or margarine
1 medium onion, finely minced
1 tablespoon dried dill or ½ cup minced fresh dill
2 (10-ounce) packages frozen artichoke hearts, thawed
2 cups converted rice
5 cups chicken broth
1 (8-ounce) can tomato sauce
¼ pound butter
Salt and pepper to taste

Melt the 4 tablespoons butter in a deep pot. Add the onion, dill, and artichokes and brown. Add the rice and allow to brown for 2 minutes. In a saucepan bring the chicken broth and tomato sauce to a boil and add to the rice and artichokes. Cover and simmer over low heat for 20 minutes, or until all water is absorbed. Brown the ¼ pound butter, pour over the rice mixture, and season with salt and pepper. Stir to blend. Remove from the heat and let stand for 5 minutes before serving.

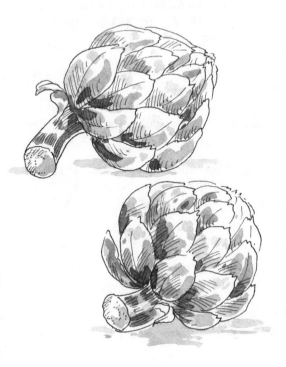

HEART OF LETTUCE AND
HEART OF ROMAINE SALAD
SALADE DE COEUR DE LAITUE ET
COEUR DE ROMAINE

SERVES 4
2 small heads lettuce and 2 small heads romaine
½ recipe French Dressing with Mustard (given below)
1 tablespoon finely minced fresh chervil and tarragon

Remove all the outer leaves to get at the hearts. Cut each heart in half lengthwise and dress with French dressing. Sprinkle the hearts with the herbs before tossing.

FRENCH DRESSING WITH MUSTARD
VINAIGRETTE MOUTARDÉE

MAKES ABOUT ½ CUP
5 tablespoons peanut oil or olive oil
Salt
1 scant tablespoon red wine vinegar
Freshly ground pepper
1 teaspoon strong Dijon mustard
1 teaspoon mild mustard

Put the oil and salt in a bowl and beat with a wire whisk. Add the vinegar, then the pepper. Mix the two mustards together, then add to the rest of the ingredients. Beat for about 50 seconds, or until the mixture is well blended and smooth.

CHESTNUT CAKE WITH WHIPPED CREAM
KASTANA TOURTA

A simplified version of a very popular—and delicious—Greek dessert.

MAKES 10–12 PIECES

6 eggs, separated
1¼ cups sugar
1 cup canned unsweetened chestnut purée
½ cup ground almonds, lightly toasted
1 teaspoon vanilla extract
Pinch salt
1½ cups heavy cream for whipping
10 ounces glacéed chestnuts (optional)

Preheat oven to 325° F. In a bowl beat the egg yolks and sugar with electric beater or a whisk until the mixture forms ribbons when the beater is lifted. Add the chestnut purée, ground almonds, and vanilla. Beat egg whites with salt until stiff. Add ¼ of the whites to the yolk mixture and combine well. Gently fold the remaining whites into the yolk mixture. Pour the batter into 2 buttered and floured 9″ cake pans and bake for 35 minutes. Let the layers cool in the pans for 15 minutes. Turn them out onto racks and cool completely. Whip the cream, fill and frost the layers with it. Decorate with glacéed chestnuts, if desired.

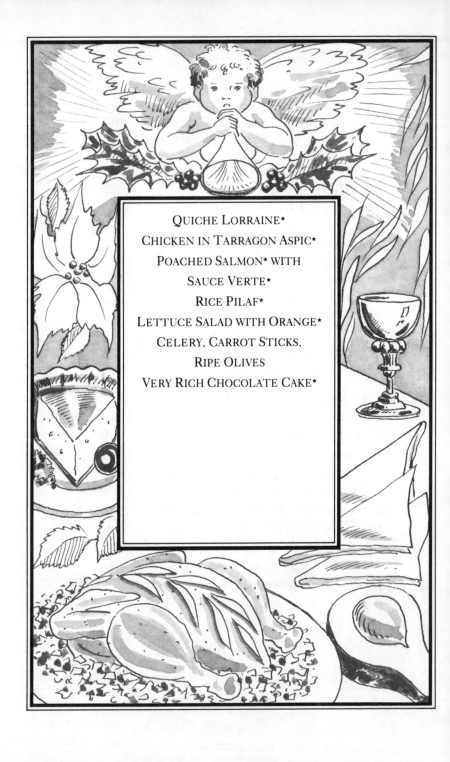

QUICHE LORRAINE⋆
CHICKEN IN TARRAGON ASPIC⋆
POACHED SALMON⋆ WITH
SAUCE VERTE⋆
RICE PILAF⋆
LETTUCE SALAD WITH ORANGE⋆
CELERY, CARROT STICKS,
RIPE OLIVES
VERY RICH CHOCOLATE CAKE⋆

New Year's
Day
Buffet

THE AUTHORS OF *The Doubleday Cookbook* have given us a quiche recipe that will especially appeal to guests who come to visit on January 1 after church or sleeping late.

QUICHE LORRAINE

SERVES 10 AS APPETIZER, 6 AS ENTREE

FLAKY PASTRY

MAKES ONE CRUST FOR 8″, 9″, OR 10″ QUICHE
1¼ cups sifted flour
½ teaspoon salt
⅓ cup chilled vegetable shortening or lard
¼ cup ice water

Place flour and salt in a shallow mixing bowl and cut in shortening with a pastry blender until mixture resembles coarse meal. Sprinkle water over surface, 1 tablespoon at a time, and mix in lightly and quickly with a fork, just until pastry holds together. Shape gently into a ball on a lightly floured pastry cloth, then flatten into a circle about 1″ thick, evening up rough edges. Using a lightly floured, stockinette-covered rolling pin and short, firm strokes, roll into a circle about 3″ larger than the pan you plan to use. To transfer pastry to pan, lay rolling pin across center of pastry circle, fold half of pastry over pin and ease into pan; press lightly. Seal any cracks or holes by pressing dampened scraps of pastry on top. Trim pastry so it hangs evenly 1″ over rim, roll overhang under even with rim and crimp or flute.

FILLING

½ pound bacon, crisply cooked and crumbled
½ pound Gruyère or Swiss cheese, coarsely grated
4 eggs, lightly beaten
1 teaspoon salt
⅛ teaspoon white pepper
Pinch cayenne pepper
⅛ teaspoon nutmeg (optional)
1¾ cups light cream
1 tablespoon melted butter

Preheat oven to 425° F. Prepare pastry, roll into a 12″ circle, and fit into a 9″ piepan, making a high, fluted edge. Prick bottom and sides of pastry well with a fork; cover with wax paper and fill with uncooked rice or dried beans. Bake 5−7 minutes until firm but not brown, then cool slightly on a wire rack. Remove paper and rice. Sprinkle bacon and cheese evenly over pie shell. Mix together remaining ingredients and strain through a fine sieve. Place pie shell on partly pulled-out oven rack, then pour in egg mixture. Bake, uncovered, 15 minutes at 425° F., reduce heat to 350° F., and bake 10−15 minutes longer or until a knife inserted halfway between center and rim comes out clean. Cool on a wire rack 8−10 minutes before cutting into wedges. Serve as an appetizer or luncheon entree.

CHICKEN IN TARRAGON ASPIC
POULET RÔTI À LA GELÉE D'ESTRAGON

SERVES 4

Salt

Freshly ground pepper

1 (2½–3-pound) roasting chicken

1–2 sprigs fresh tarragon (or 1 teaspoon dried)

2–3 pats butter

Butter for the roasting pan

3 cups clarified jellied chicken consommé (recipe given below); set ½ cup aside for chopped aspic garnish

½ cup red port wine or dry sherry

4 tablespoons warmed cognac flamed in a ladle

12 fresh tarragon leaves, scalded, refreshed, and patted dry, for decoration

Preheat oven to 375° F. Salt and pepper the inside of the chicken. Slip the sprigs of tarragon and pats of butter in the cavity. Truss the chicken and set it breast up in a well-buttered roasting pan. Brown the breast and both sides, seasoning lightly with salt and pepper each time you turn it. Place the chicken on its back and roast for about 1 hour, or until juices run a clear amber color when the thick part of a leg is pricked. Prepare the aspic while the chicken is roasting.

TO PREPARE THE ASPIC

Heat the consommé, stir in one of the wines, add the flamed cognac, and adjust seasoning. The consommé should be very well seasoned, as it loses some of its aromatic taste as it turns to jelly. Cool and place in the refrigerator until it has the consistency of thick syrup.

TO PREPARE THE CHOPPED ASPIC
FOR GARNISHING

Put the reserved ½ cup of jellied consommé in a square pan (the jelly should be about ½ inch thick). Place in the refrigerator until completely set. Just before using it as decoration, chop it into small pieces with a sharp knife.

TO PREPARE THE CHICKEN

Cut the legs and wings from the roast chicken. Remove the breast, trimming away the cartilage, cut it in half with poultry shears. Place the chicken on its back upon an oval platter. Using this as a base, reconstruct the chicken as far as possible in its original form, using wooden toothpicks for holding the pieces together until the first coating of jelly has set. Decorate the chicken with a herringbone pattern of tarragon leaves, pushing them into the skin so they stick.

When the chicken is completely cool, brush it with a layer of jelly, refrigerate until the jelly has set. Remove the toothpicks, brush the chicken with another coating of jelly, and replace in the refrigerator. Repeat the process 2 more times, refrigerating after each layer of jelly has been added. Keep the chicken in the refrigerator until ready to serve.

Just before serving, ring the platter with the ice-cold chopped aspic.

CHICKEN BOUILLON
BOUILLON DE VOLAILLE

Use 3½ quarts of water to obtain 2½ quarts of finished bouillon, for use in the recipe for chicken consommé, given below.

1 (4-pound) stewing hen, cleaned and dressed
3½ quarts warm water
1 bouquet garni
1 onion, peeled and quartered
1 carrot, peeled, scraped, and cut in 2 lengthwise
Salt
Freshly ground pepper

Place the hen in a large, heavy-bottomed enameled kettle, pour in the water, and gradually bring to a boil. Add the *bouquet garni* and all the rest of the ingredients. Simmer for 2–2½ hours. Adjust for seasoning. Remove chicken. Degrease and strain the broth through a sieve lined with dampened cheesecloth.

CHICKEN CONSOMMÉ
CONSOMMÉ DE VOLAILLE

2½ quarts chicken bouillon (see preceding recipe)
Raw giblets of 2 chickens
1 bouquet garni *(with fresh chervil and fresh tarragon if possible)*
The white of half a leek

Simmer these ingredients slowly for 35–40 minutes, degrease, and put through a sieve lined with dampened cheesecloth. For clarifying the consommé, see following recipe.

CLARIFYING CONSOMMÉ

This method of clarification is astonishing and may be called a triumph of kitchen chemistry. It is always a good idea to clarify consommés, and when these are to be served jellied, the method is indispensable.

1¾–2¼ quarts cold consommé
2–3 egg whites (to which a crushed eggshell may be added)
1 small stalk celery or some green from a leek, chopped
2–3 finely minced sprigs fresh chervil
2–3 finely minced sprigs fresh tarragon

Pour 2 ladlefuls of cold consommé into a bowl. Add the egg whites and beat vigorously until frothy. Then, using a fork, beat in the vegetable and herbs. Pour the remaining cold consommé into a large, heavy-bottomed enameled kettle and set over moderate heat. Beat in the contents of the bowl. Continue beating until the liquid begins to boil. During this procedure you will be aghast to see (if you are a novice) that the liquid has become cloudy and full of impurities. But as the heat intensifies, all these impurities will rise and form a layer of scum on top of the consommé. Continue beating. At a certain point a crack will appear in the scum, and it is at this moment that you stop beating. Boil for one minute to solidify the scum. Remove the kettle from the heat.

Dampen a piece of cheesecloth, wring it out, and line a large strainer with it. Place the strainer over a large bowl. Remove part of the solidified scum with a skimmer and strain the consommé into the bowl. The crystal-clear result will astonish the cook who has performed this operation for the first time.

If you wish to improve the bouquet of the consommé, add ½ cup Madeira or ½ cup dry sherry to each quart of soup.

POACHED SALMON

SERVES 6−8

2 quarts water
1½ cups dry white wine
2 bay leaves
1 sprig fresh parsley
1 stalk celery
3 sprigs fresh dill or ¼ teaspoon dill seed
1 sprig fresh thyme or pinch dried thyme
1 small yellow onion, peeled and quartered
10 peppercorns, bruised
1 teaspoon salt
1 (5-pound) center-cut piece fresh salmon, cleaned and dressed

Boil all ingredients except salmon, uncovered, 25 minutes and strain through a double thickness of cheesecloth. Wipe salmon with damp cloth and wrap in a double thickness of cheesecloth. Place in a large oval kettle on a rack so that loose cheesecloth ends are on top. Pour in strained liquid, cover, and simmer 40 minutes (liquid should never boil). Lift rack and salmon from kettle, remove cheesecloth, peel off skin, and carefully scrape away any darkened flesh. Cool to room temperature and chill 8 – 10 hours. Serve with Sauce Verte (recipe follows).

SAUCE VERTE

MAKES ABOUT 2½ CUPS
1 recipe Homemade Mayonnaise (given below)
¼ cup minced fresh spinach
¼ cup minced watercress leaves
¼ cup minced fresh parsley
2 tablespoons minced chives
2 tablespoons water
1 teaspoon minced fresh tarragon (½ teaspoon dried)

Prepare mayonnaise as directed below and set aside. Place ¼ cup each minced fresh spinach, watercress leaves, and parsley in a small pan, add the chives, water, and tarragon, cover, and simmer 2 minutes. Press mixture through a fine sieve, drain briefly, and blend into mayonnaise. Serve with the poached salmon.

HOMEMADE MAYONNAISE

Mayonnaise isn't tricky to make—*if* you follow these basic rules:

—Have all ingredients at room temperature before beginning.

—Measure oil accurately into a wide-mouthed container so you can dip it out by spoonfuls during early stages of mixing.

—If mixing by hand, place a damp cloth under bowl to keep it from sliding around as you mix. Use a fork or wire whisk for beating.

—Add oil in the beginning *by the drop* so that it will emulsify with the egg yolks.

—If you substitute vinegar for lemon juice, use the very finest quality so mayonnaise will have a delicate flavor.

—*If mayonnaise separates, use 1 of the following remedies:*

　　—Beat in 1−2 teaspoons hot water.

　　—Beat 1 egg yolk with 2 or 3 drops oil until very thick, then beat in curdled mayonnaise drop by drop.

　　—Buzz in an electric blender at high speed.

MAYONNAISE

MAKES 1½ CUPS

2 egg yolks
¾ teaspoon salt
½ teaspoon powdered mustard
⅛ teaspoon sugar
Pinch cayenne pepper
4−5 teaspoons lemon juice or white vinegar
1½ cups olive or other salad oil
4 teaspoons hot water

Beat yolks, salt, mustard, sugar, pepper, and 1 teaspoon lemon juice in a small bowl until very thick and pale yellow. (Note: If using electric mixer, beat at medium speed.) Add about ¼ cup oil, drop by drop, beating vigorously all the while. Beat in 1 teaspoon each lemon juice and hot water. Add another ¼ cup oil, a few drops at a time, beating vigorously all the while. Beat in another teaspoon each lemon juice and water. Add ½ cup oil in a very fine steady stream, beating constantly, then mix in remaining lemon juice and water; slowly beat in remaining oil. If you like, thin mayonnaise with a little additional hot water. Cover and refrigerate until needed. (Note: Store in warmest part of refrigerator—less chance of the mayonnaise's separating—and do not keep longer than one week.)

Variation

Blender Mayonnaise: Place yolks, salt, mustard, sugar, pepper, and 3 teaspoons lemon juice in blender cup and buzz at low speed 15 seconds. Increase speed to moderately high and slowly drizzle in ¼ cup oil. As mixture begins to thicken, continue adding oil in a fine steady stream, alternating with hot water and remaining lemon juice. Stop blender and scrape mixture down from sides as needed.

RICE PILAF

SERVES 4
¼ cup butter or margarine
1 cup uncooked rice
2 cups hot chicken or beef broth
½ teaspoon salt (about)
⅛ teaspoon pepper

Melt butter in a heavy saucepan over moderately low heat, add rice, and stir-fry about 5 minutes until straw-colored. Add broth, salt, and pepper, cover, and cook over lowest heat without stirring 18–20 minutes until all liquid is absorbed. Uncover and cook 3–5 minutes longer to dry out. Fluff with a fork, taste for salt, and adjust as needed.

LETTUCE SALAD WITH ORANGE
SALADE DE LAITUE À L'ORANGE

SERVES 6
2 large heads lettuce
1 large healthy orange

DRESSING FOR THE SALAD

4 tablespoons peanut oil or olive oil
Juice of ½ orange
*1–2 tablespoons lemon juice (amount depends on acidity of
    orange juice)*
Salt
Freshly ground pepper

Wash, trim, and drain well the lettuce leaves, put

them in a shallow salad bowl. With a lemon peeler remove the rind from the orange and cut the rind into slivers. Remove the pith from the orange with a sharp knife. Cut the orange into sections. Mix the dressing ingredients together, beat, and pour over the lettuce leaves. Garnish with orange sections and slivered peel.

VERY RICH CHOCOLATE CAKE

SERVES 10—12
½ pound mild chocolate
½ pound dark sweet chocolate
4 tablespoons flour
3 tablespoons sugar
1½ sticks sweet butter, softened and cut up
4 eggs, separated

Preheat oven to 450° F. Melt chocolate in top of double boiler over barely simmering water. Stir in the flour, sugar, and butter. Beat the egg yolks well and stir into the chocolate mixture; cool. Whip the egg whites until stiff and fold into the batter. Pour into a greased, paper-lined 8-inch square cake pan and bake 15 minutes; cool in the pan, then unmold. This cake can be frosted with a rich chocolate-butter icing an inch thick, but it really needs no gilding. Proceed at your figure's own risk. This is a supermoist cake— almost the consistency of baked custard.

SOUR CREAM AND POTATO SOUP★
CORN BREAD MUFFINS
BAKED HOME-CURED HAM★ WITH
WINE-RAISIN SAUCE★
SUPERB SWEET POTATOES★
TURNIPS, RUTABAGA, AND
KOHLRABI★
WALDORF SALAD★
FUNNY PIE★
VANILLA ICE CREAM

Twelfth
Night
Supper

MUCH OF THIS MEAL can be cooked in the oven. The heat from the stove will help to warm your kitchen, and the vegetables and other foods may all be found at the market.

Waldorf Salad is one I have been making since I was in high school. Almost everyone is familiar with it since it is a very simple recipe. Just apples, celery, nuts, the mayonnaise. It is very good for wintertime salads, and you are sure to enjoy it. Funny Pie is very good with this dinner. This meal should warm up your family by the fireside.

from BETTY GROFF'S COUNTRY GOODNESS COOKBOOK

SOUR CREAM AND POTATO SOUP

SERVES 4–6
2 tablespoons butter, margarine, or bacon fat
¼ cup chopped onion
¾ cup chopped celery
4 medium white potatoes, peeled and cut into strips, as for julienne
2 whole cloves or ¼ teaspoon grated nutmeg
1½ teaspoons salt

5 cups water
2 tablespoons all-purpose flour
¼ cup water
½ cup sour cream
Freshly ground pepper for garnish

Melt the shortening in a soup kettle. Add the onion and the celery. Sauté until lightly browned. Add the potatoes, cloves, salt, and 5 cups water. Cover and cook approximately 15 minutes until potatoes are tender. Moisten the flour with ¼ cup water to make a smooth paste. Add to thicken the soup slightly. In a separate bowl, remove 1 cup of the soup and gently combine with the sour cream. Return to the soup kettle and heat. Do not bring to a boil, or the sour cream will separate. Serve in heated soup bowls and add pepper for garnish.

BAKED HOME-CURED HAM

SERVES 12

1 (12–14-pound) whole smoked, cured ham
2 cups water

Remove the rind from the cured ham and place, bone side down, in a roaster pan. Add water, tent with foil, and bake in a 300° F. preheated oven for 2½ hours. Remove and debone. If the broth seems salty, pour off and add 2 cups fresh water. Put the deboned ham in the water and continue to bake at 300° F. for another hour. Serve plain or with Wine-Raisin Sauce.

Baking the ham in water keeps it moist and tender. Changing the water is necessary only if the ham is very salty. It will still retain the smoky flavor.

WINE-RAISIN SAUCE

ENOUGH FOR ABOUT 12

2½ cups dry red or white wine
1 cup sugar
2 tablespoons prepared mustard
½ teaspoon salt
1 cup raisins
2 tablespoons arrowroot dissolved in ¼ cup water

In a 2-quart saucepan, stir the wine, sugar, mustard, and salt with a wire whip until well mixed. Add the raisins. Simmer on low heat for 30 minutes. Add the dissolved arrowroot to the sauce. Return to a boil and simmer 1 minute until thickened.

SUPERB SWEET POTATOES

SERVES 6

Next to plain buttered sweet potatoes, this recipe is the best! So often, sweet potatoes are ruined when the cook uses too much sugar, pineapple, and marshmallows. Folding in the whipped cream makes the sweet potatoes light and fluffy without being overpowering. This recipe blends well with any meal, and the topping adds a special touch.

2 pounds (about 6 medium) sweet potatoes, orange, yellow,
*   or white*
4 cups water
2 teaspoons salt
2 tablespoons butter

Freshly ground black pepper to taste
¼–½ cup scalded milk, depending on type of sweet potatoes
used
1 cup chilled heavy cream
¼ cup brown sugar

Wash the unpeeled sweet potatoes. Cook in a large saucepan in the water with 1 teaspoon salt for about 20 minutes until tender but not mushy. Drain, peel, and mash to a purée. This may be done in a food processor, blender, or electric mixer. Add the remaining salt, butter, pepper, and milk. For white sweet potatoes, which are drier, you will need ½ cup milk, but if you use the moist orange type, often sold as yams (which they are not, just another type of sweet potato), use only ¼ cup. Beat until smooth and fluffy. Whip the chilled cream in a chilled bowl (this helps it to thicken faster). Fold half of the whipped cream gently into the potato mixture, and put in a buttered 1½–2-quart casserole. Top with the rest of the whipped cream and sprinkle with the brown sugar. Bake in a preheated 375° F. oven for 20–25 minutes until golden brown.

TURNIPS, RUTABAGA, AND KOHLRABI

SERVES 6

All of these vegetables are reasonably priced in season, yet seldom used. I hope this recipe will encourage you to try them. All of them retain their colors well when they are cooked, and are pleasing to the eye when sliced, diced, and cubed.

1 pound kohlrabi, peeled and cubed
1 pound rutabaga, peeled and sliced
½ pound white turnips, peeled and diced
2 cups beef stock
Salt
Freshly ground pepper

Put the vegetables and beef stock in a 3-quart sauce-pan, cover, and cook about 25 minutes over medium heat until tender. Check for seasoning, and add salt and freshly ground pepper as needed, depending on the seasoning in the beef stock.

WALDORF SALAD

SERVES 6
2 cups diced whole red apples
1 cup chopped celery
½ cup broken nuts
½ cup mayonnaise
Fresh lettuce leaves
Nut halves or maraschino cherries for garnish

Combine the apples, celery, nuts, and mayonnaise gently in a large bowl. Chill in the refrigerator until ready to serve. Serve on crisp lettuce leaves. Garnish with nut halves or maraschino cherries.

FUNNY PIE

MAKES 2 (9″) PIES
Sallie Harner, of Cincinnati, sent me this recipe for Funny Pie. It is a take-off on Shoofly Pie, with a chocolate rather than a molasses base. Sallie's family used to live in Bucks County. Funny Pie is as popular with the

Pennsylvania Dutch in that area as Shoofly Pie is with us.

LIQUID BOTTOM MIXTURE

1 cup granulated sugar
½ teaspoon salt
½ cup cocoa
¾ cup hot water
1 teaspoon vanilla extract

BATTER FOR TOPPING

½ cup butter, at room temperature
2 cups granulated sugar
2 eggs
2 cups flour
½ teaspoon salt
2 teaspoons baking powder
1 cup milk
¾ teaspoon vanilla extract
2 unbaked 9" pie shells

To make the bottom, stir the sugar, salt, and cocoa together in a saucepan. Slowly add the hot water and blend until smooth. Bring to a boil and simmer for 5 minutes. Remove from the heat and add the vanilla. Cool while preparing batter for topping.

Cream the butter and sugar in a mixing bowl. Beat in the eggs, 1 at a time. Sift the flour, salt, and baking powder into another bowl. Gradually beat into the butter-sugar-egg mixture, alternately with the milk, until smooth. Add the vanilla.

Pour the cooled liquid bottom mixture into the unbaked pie shells. Drop the batter evenly over it. Bake in a preheated 375° F. oven for 50–60 minutes until the filling is firm when the pan is moved.

INDEX